'It' is GOLD
Ellie Ann Deighton

Copyright © 2025 by Ellie Ann Deighton

All rights reserved.

No part of this publication may be reproduced, distributed, or transmitted in any form or by any means, including photocopying, recording, or other electronic or mechanical methods, without the prior written permission of the publisher, except as permitted by Australian copyright law. For permission requests or bulk orders, contact the author.

The story, all names, characters, and incidents portrayed in this production are fictitious. No identification with actual persons (living or deceased), places, buildings, and products is intended or should be inferred.

Book Cover by Ellie Ann Deighton

1st Edition 2025

Contents

Epigraph	1
Ellie's Gold	2
Dedication	4
Foreword	9
1. It is an unknown thing.	13
2. It is a discovery.	45
3. It is yours for the taking.	63
4. It is gold.	99
Wishing Gold	127
fire body warm	135
About the author	137
Author's note	139
Acknowledgements	141

Gold is inside all of us inherently. It is part of being human. We all have a golden thread in our heart that is our greatness, our genius.
Connecting to, living, being guided by the gold leads to a most flourishing and deeply love-filled expression of life.
~ evidence suggests

ELLIE WRITES LOTS OF GOLD

FICTION
Ankhara Codes I: An Adventure to Essence
Ankhara Codes II: Allies of the Soul
Ankhara Codes III: A Devotion To Peace

ORACLE CARDS
Fruits of the Feminine

POETRY
fire body warm
water river run

NON-FICTION
Myths of a Mystic Woman

JOURNAL
Creatively Loving

MUSIC ALBUMS
Temple Calling: An Album For Your Altar
Heart Calling: A Love Anthology (coming 2025)

ONLINE TRAININGS & COURSES:
Intuitively Me: The Wheel of Life

more at elliedeighton.com

This is the first book of seven in The Elemental Collection; a poetry series focused on the seven essential elements of fulfilment.

You can read The Elemental Collection in any order you choose.

A Mysterious Dedication

This book I write to set me free,
From all that 'I' isn't and all that I've been
This book I am writing to hear that sweet voice
That tells me sweet stories in that sweet gentle voice
And always guides home to the voice of my heart
And helps show me where when I forget how to start
I'm writing this book for the girl who remembers
And no one will tell her anything except forgetting
I'm writing this book for the little girl to dance
So she may be seen as sunshine and rainbows
And given her every chance
To express and laugh and cry and be heard
And be held across the table as she explores the essence of her world
And flies through sacred stables
Some that frighten her, scare her, some that help her see
That her gift is freely giving and freely giving is really free
And only free if it's from a space that is full
It's expensive if it is not
These words will remind her of who she is not so she can then dance on the table
No longer questioning
Doubting
Or visioning
A blur that is not really hers.
She will see
Crystal clear

'IT' IS GOLD

Like a giant crystal ball
Her magic
Her bliss
Her true speaking.
A romance in the evening
And a deluge in the morning
It's a delicacy at the dining table
And a taste of all the fawning
It is yes and no and maybe and sometimes
But always just under the surface
And if you let it
If you whisper it in
You'll feel its truest service
It's a filter
An aura
An energy field
An insect that falls through isn't able
To do any harm
Or make any mistake
It's all part of your gifts on the table.
So open it up
Open eyes, hands and heart
And see what becomes available
When only you ask
And only you let
Your true voice unveil your true fable
It's a magic that beats
Silver finery down the street and you cannot sweep the pulsing away

ELLIE ANN DEIGHTON

It's a magic that keeps
Beating under your feet
Even when your mind tells it to stray
It cannot be dampened
Or settled into difference
Because there is just no such thing
It's right there right here now
If only you'll listen
Your brilliant true song will now sing
And bam
There you are
Now I see you and feel
The essence of your magic
And oh lord, by God, it's real
Please shine the light
And keep it on
No matter what will face you
Because even the darkest depths of Avalon mists
Cannot ruin the love of this space
This space in your heart that radiates gentle bliss
And kisses the faces of strangers
It dances between us and lands underneath us
And with this, love, the truth is there is no real danger.

Can you imagine awakening from a dream only to read the poetry that your sleeping self wrote? Well, I couldn't either. Then I did, and this book was born.

'IT' IS GOLD

I dedicate this book to the mysterious gold, the well-known gold, the familiar gold, the untouched gold, the sacred gold, all the gold in me and all the gold in you.

May you read this book to remember

To relish

To be relentless

In gold.

ELLIE ANN DEIGHTON

Foreword

In my journal I wrote...

October 5 2020

End result: To meet my muse and be informed of the calling of my heart.

I am the magic
And the muse
And I am here
To say to you:

It's time to shine.
No ifs or buts,
It's time to divine
What makes you alive.
The thing that brought
You to Earth for a reason
The thing that you felt
Was your life purpose season.

That's why I'm here;
To share you and your gifts
To create space that anchors you
So that perhaps you'll shift
And you'll no longer pretend
That you are here for free,
You'll quit that and start remembering
You're here for you and me.
You're here for spreading a magic
That only you can feel and handle
And you're here to paint the skies with colours
That drip down sides of candles
And you're here
Despite your resistance (or not)
To come home to this essence
And whether you love it
Hate it
Wish it different or better,
You're here to share your presence
And your presence is special
It's true, it's unique
There's no sideways one or two about it.
There's no oblong or oblique
Shape that takes away
From the brilliance of who you are
And if you let it,
If you let me stay,
I'll remind you of the stars

The very stars from which you came
When you fell down to Earth.
It's not a trick or special place for some
It's the reason you were birthed
And it's the reason you're right here right now
So you can pause, stop and see
That if you forget your magic another minute
That means forgetting me.
That means forgetting this magical moment
And all the bliss that comes with it,
That means forgetting the ways that you want it
And letting yourself live in fear of it.
It means letting go of your gifts and your art
And hiding among old dusty paintings and frames
And that, miss or sir or master or mistress,
Is not at all why to Earth you came;
You came here to shine
To spread love on this planet
Yes, in your own special way.
And no, it's not silly,
It's your unique talent
And that is where joy comes to stay.
That is where magic and mastery can happen
Alive in all that is sacred
In all you'd wish, with romance, with kisses
And golden leaves for the table.
It's not limited
And neither are you

Your expression is right here for the taking
And if you read on,
One more page, one more chapter
Forgetting is what you're forsaking.

Welcome to Gold.

It is an unknown thing.

'You have ugly alien feet,'
Said my friend
And I laughed it off
Because it was confusing.
But it wasn't really confusing
It hurt
– And suddenly my body wasn't gold

'IT' IS GOLD

'We're not going to see Poppy today,'
Said my dad
And I frown
Because of course we are going,
That's what we are doing today.
But we aren't
– He died and the world felt grey

There isn't anything
Anyone can say
To talk me out of
How green the trees are
And how magical this forest is
Where the trains used to be
And the fairies still are
And the tree people whisper
And my friends share my imagination
But I swear
It isn't in our imaginations
It's real
– The world is gold

'IT' IS GOLD

I don't imagine
What it might be like
If the sun didn't rise one morning
But I bet it would be beautiful
– Because everything is always okay when the world is gold

I'm pretty sure
He wasn't supposed to wake me up
But he did
And now he's crying
And I don't know if little girls
Cherish their dads like I do
But I do
– I'll hold him until he remembers the gold

'IT' IS GOLD

I love people
I love that other little girls have birthdays
And I get to test drive their birthday bikes
Because this is the *most fun I've ever had*
And I'm pretty sure that I'm not riding a bike
I'm riding a unicorn
– It was gold *before* I found out it was mine

I simply cannot imagine

Why someone might be mean to their friends

Regularly

I did it once

And I felt so sick I couldn't go to school

And I had to talk to the teacher

About how little girls aren't meant to be little bitches

We are meant to be little girls

It hurt me to hurt her

And I think it hurt her to hurt me too

– There's a blended world of beige and gold and some days I don't know which I'm in but one of them really hurts

'IT' IS GOLD

'Give us your money!'
He is stealing
From me and my big brother
And big brother says no
Big brother is brave
But I'm scared
So I hold out my hand
Coins offered for the vending machine
– Fear makes you forget the gold

Maybe they need it more than me.
If they climb to my room
On the third floor
To enter through my unlocked balcony door
And steal my belongings
And maybe I won't notice
If they hurt me
So I'll leave the door unlocked
Everything is fine
– Too much fake gold, delusional gold

Everything is fine
Everything is fine
Everything is fine
My fingers curl so tightly
Everything is fine
My eyes hurt from crying
I'm not fine
But I have to be
– I can't remember the gold

Maybe there isn't good left in me anymore
Maybe I hurt too many people
Maybe that's why my brother won't play with me
Maybe that's why he won't let me near his friends
Maybe
– He forgot his friends are gold, not just me

'IT' IS GOLD

He's on the floor
My other brother
From another mother
Is on top of him
We only kissed
I'm only eighteen today
I want to be kissed
We're running out the door
We're in a taxi
We're leaving under the influence
I can't remember what happened
– There's gold in everything, right?

Maybe not all of the teachers see me like I do
'Did you use a ruler? That's incredibly straight!'
I drew the sign for our hot-glue-gun stick house
'Nope!'
I smile.
I'm proud.
He frowns and walks off.
– Why can't he see my gold?

'IT' IS GOLD

There's a big bump on the back of the van
Over where the tyre goes
I can sit on it while he drives across the oval
It's against the rules!
I laugh
It's fun!
My dad is the best
– Not all rules are golden

My mum fills up the water bottles
For my brother's whole team
And washes towels
And washes uniforms
And so much holding
She does a lot of holding
They're treated like they're old
But they're young
She loves them with all her heart and soul
They smile at her right into their eyes
– Gold eases the pressures

'At least when you miss your mum she's helping people,'
I tell my friend.
Her mum is a shift nurse.
She doesn't see her much.
– I'm trying to find the gold

'It doesn't matter on the farm!'
Kids can't drive
But here they do
You shouldn't scratch cars
But here they do
I'd get in trouble
But here they don't
I'm scared
They love it
Is that okay?
'Don't tell my mum.'
– Different people have different gold

'IT' IS GOLD

I'm getting laughed at,
Because I didn't hear.
I didn't hear my name.

'Most Valuable Player of the Season is Ellie Deighton'

Someone touches me
Interrupts my focus
What? I'm studying chemistry, leave me be
'Ellie, you won!'
I won a trophy
I'm standing up embarrassed,
They're laughing at me for being in my book,
They think I'm a nerd,
I don't belong here,
I'm not a jock
– They weren't laughing at my gold

'You got the most votes, but you won't be the head girl.'
'We need to share the leadership positions.'
They want fair
I want a life of gold
Ultimately,
I'm the winner.
They forgot gold is the truest prize
– Gold isn't fair, it's true

'IT' IS GOLD

The swimming pool
Seems like a good place to start writing poems
I'll write them
And share them
With a select few
– Unsure of my writing gold

'Write a book!'
Says my intuition
'That's a bit of a big ask'
Says my self doubt.
– Intuition has the gold

'What's your book going to be about?'
I've got no idea.
'It doesn't matter,'
Said the gold.
'Writing it is what matters.'
– Following the gold is the only goal

I tried to help him write a book
I wrote them down
Thousands of words
While he spoke them
While we lived them
He never published
I have six now
– One of us followed the gold

'IT' IS GOLD

He would make love to me
But he wouldn't choose me
He would take me for dinner
Date me
Bed me
But he'd never wed me
– It wasn't gold

She sees me in ways I've never been seen

She chooses me

She tried to kiss me

I ducked

– Terrified of the purest gold

'IT' IS GOLD

If love is love

And I can have anything

Then why do I think love is love when it's for everyone else

And nothing is ever enough

When it's me

— I don't trust the gold when I see it

I thought we could just be friends
Grab coffee
I could come over
Care about you
– I'm more gold than my sex

'IT' IS GOLD

I thought I knew gold
I thought I was gold
I thought we were gold
Why'd you die?
– Everything *has* gold, not everything *is* gold

I was born
And I was a star
And I didn't know it
And I did
And they didn't know it
And they did
– When did we all forget the gold?

'IT' IS GOLD

It seems a weird age

Every age

It's different to how I thought the age would be

Why do we care so much?

When all our ages are different?

My six is different to yours,

So is my seven,

I might not get a seventy,

You already did,

Why does it matter?

Why do I care so much?

– Gold isn't measured in years but we think it is

ELLIE ANN DEIGHTON

It is a discovery.

'I want to help people when I grow up,'
I'd tell anyone who listened
But I didn't listen
Not to me
I listened to them
I listened to what they said helping people looked like
I tried to become a doctor
It wasn't right
I felt selfish
Because I was great
But I wasn't happy
I felt there was more
I couldn't explain it
I simply knew
'I'm going to help people when I grow up'
It was true
But this wasn't the way
– It wasn't the greatest gold for me

'IT' IS GOLD

People stay with you
And people judge you
And both are okay
– You follow your gold and others will leave and it's good gold

I'm here now
I missed a flight
And it feels right
It's a mystery
I didn't plan this
I think that's the point
– Gold lives in the unexpected

'IT' IS GOLD

I didn't come alone
Even though I did
I knew people here
And that made it easier
Even though I'm solely here for me
And in my life I'll always be alone
In my life there will always be people
And people make it easier
– I've discovered the gold in a teacher who believes in me

'Wow, I wish I'd discovered this at your age.'
They said at the tantra retreat
They said at the concert
They said at the workshop
They said
They said
They said
Focusing on me
All the while missing their own discoveries
– Gold is there if you're looking for it

Maybe we don't go that way
Maybe we do
We don't usually go that way
– Gold isn't boring

We're in a pattern

We have a fight

I feel terrible

He's annoyed

I want to reconnect

He wants to avoid

We're in a pattern

This pattern sucks

We can't get over it

Now we just fuck

It doesn't make sense

How did we get here?

We shouldn't be here anymore

Break up

Leave

It's over

There

– Gold shrinks when you insist on avoiding it

'IT' IS GOLD

'Have you ever considered that you created this?'
He asks.
He looks like he feels bad.
Pity in his eyes.
But why would he say that?
Anger in my everything
Freezing in my cells
I wouldn't choose that
I wouldn't choose that
I wouldn't choose that
The worst thing that could ever happen
It happened
I couldn't create that
And if I'm honest
I did
And I liked that it proved all the black, grey and beige things about me
to be true
I create the magic
And I created this deep dark blue
– Gold is acknowledging that you create it all

What if

I could choose to be happy?

What if

I could choose how to respond?

What if

I could gift random acts of kindness?

What if

Abundance was a feeling beyond a bank account?

What if

I didn't need to know everything?

What if

I did it even if they said I was crazy?

What if

Everything was a choice?

– You can choose more gold

'IT' IS GOLD

He was always kind to me
Believed in my dreams
Even respected them

When others shunned me for it.
He got the way I lived better than anyone else I went to school with.
Why do the masculine figures always seem to die?
– Gold isn't what everyone chooses and it'll never make sense

'Are you okay?'

Because I'm sober

Because I'm 'different'

Because I moved away

Because I chose to leave

Because university wasn't working for me

Because my heart broke

Because I didn't keep up with communications

Because I'm happy and they can't see

– It takes feeling the gold to see the gold

'IT' IS GOLD

It's not my strong suit
Text messages
Or emails
Or phone calls
Or distance relationships of any sort
But what is my strong suit
Is my heart
And oh I might not see you
And oh I might not speak to you
But oh
I love you
Oh how I love you
Oh and you are always welcome here
– Gold isn't conditional

It didn't happen in a moment
It happened gradually
We were friends
I thought we were
And then she didn't answer
Over and over
Missed my wedding
Stopped trying
Suddenly I hear from a friend
'I'm sorry you're not friends anymore'
The first I'm hearing
It didn't happen in a moment
Until it did
– Living gold repels the broken (or heals it if we let it)

'IT' IS GOLD

You have to let it
The gold
And sometimes you don't want to
And sometimes it seemingly sucks
Because it's uncomfortable
Stretching into who you've never been
But really it isn't
Really every time you listen to it
Follow it
Leap with it
The gold is a penny making machine
Freedom making machine
Joy making machine
Friendship making machine
Anything you were born for making machine
And now I know that
Now we know that
We have no excuse not to leap
– I've found the gold

I beat her
And it feels good
But I thought it would feel better
I saw her disappointment
And then she looked at my socks
They have the letters W A
For Western Australia
They're state socks and all the jock kids know 'em
They're also the comfiest
I wear them because I'm proud
She saw them and her eyes lit up
'You run for state?'
She asks.
'Great job!'
She compliments me before I answer.
'No.'
Her face drops.
'Basketball,'
I say with a sheepish smile
Puffing
I beat her at her game
And even though it's not my game
Running has always been my game
So why does beating her feel so bad?
– Gold isn't a people pleaser

'We're family now,'
Says Coach at the end of the championships.
He means it.
'I mean it,
No matter what,
If it's thirty years from now,
Whatever is going on in life,
We are family,
You can call me,'
He meant it.
I never tested it
Not yet
But I knew
And sometimes it's nice knowing
– Gold is people in your corner

It is yours for the taking.

I want to remind you,
'It' is yours for the taking.
It doesn't matter what 'it' is.
If you can sleeping dream 'it', you can waking dream 'it'.
If you can feel 'it', you can birth 'it'. You can live 'it'.
You had the idea because you are equipped with the vessel to birth 'it'.
You had it in the moment, Gold knew you were ready for 'it'.
Your fears and doubts are doorways and windows to the next version of you.
The struggles don't have to be what you choose.
'It' is yours for the taking,
Whatever 'it' is.
Your vision.
Your passion.
Your intention.
'It' is yours.
Don't be greedy though, honour 'it'.
If you don't allow 'it', someone else will.
This waterfall of divinity wanting to birth through you will birth through someone eventually.
So, empty.
Let it be you.
Allow 'it'.
Allow yourself the freedom of creating as a channel of your truth.
Of our truth.
Of 'its' truth.
Let 'it' be your boss.
Let 'it' declare your work hours.

Let 'it' inspire your holidays, taken because they excite you, not because you need to get away from the 'not it'.
Allowing yourself to take 'it', to birth 'it', to live by 'it', is your greatest right-now bliss.
It's your greatest service to the fire in your heart and the knowing in your gut.
It's your right-now mission.
It's your right-now measure of alignment.
Are you allowing 'it'?
Or are you squishing 'it'?
Are you choosing 'it'?
Or are you killing 'it', by prioritising the 'not it'?
Are you waiting for permission?
'It' is the permission.
Are you waiting to be ready?
 'It' is ready.
Are you waiting to feel more whole?
 'It' is both whole and holy.
There is allowing 'it'
OR
there is doing 'not it'.
So take 'it', and give yourself that long awaited ticket to fly.
'It' is worth it.
And so are you.
See what we did there?
You're worth 'it'.
'It' is your Genius and you are here to bring clarity to a life based on

'it'.
– What my muse says about gold

'IT' IS GOLD

I can see it there
The opportunity
The expert to ask
Also a friend
But I wonder
Dare I?
Dare I not?
I haven't decided.
Eventually I will.
– But why wait for the gold?

It terrifies me
To leap and to listen
To bare my soul
Completely
What if I don't glisten?
And what if I do...?
There's a little voice
A whisper
All your dreams are true for you
– There's that gold again

'IT' IS GOLD

There's a piano
And I lose myself
I don't know what I'm saying
Or who is saying it
But I know if I record it
It is medicine
I'll listen to for weeks
Healing medicine
Putting me together again
Wondrous medicine
Rifting and stitching my heart
Glorious medicine
Love never tears us apart
No,
Love is medicine
Sometimes I share the love
And always
Tears
Smiles
Perfect timing
I love the piano
– Your gold is gold for others

There's a noise

That tells me not to

I'm not good enough

I'm not worthy

I don't belong here

Women can't

I can't

People can't

Maybe another day

Eventually perhaps

I suck

Tears are a good reason not to

Never mind the true love

People will see me

Oh no

People will really see me

I'll die

– Gold can be silent and deadly and it can be a good death

'IT' IS GOLD

I'm in the sunset
Can't quite see the stars
Clouds like cotton candy
To the next adventure
Heart loud in my chest
Everything coming together
People fly in skies now
I'm one of them
– Travel is gold and this used to be the future

I couldn't receive it
Not publicly
Nor with witnesses
The upper class
Choosing to put myself there
To splurge
And then make it a new normal
'No more economy'
My soul whispered
'They'll see my success and hate me'
My fear screamed!
For a while there my fear won
I didn't tell anyone
I learned my lesson
– Hiding gold takes the shine off it
– There's no shame in gold
– Gold says have what you'd love
– Hiding pleasures and joyful secrets are very different
– Gold is the greatest teacher

I'm allowed to be happy
– Happiness is golden

ELLIE ANN DEIGHTON

Where did the good go?
– Put the golden glasses back on

'IT' IS GOLD

Seeing gold doesn't stop you
From seeing red
Or blue
Or rainbows of colours
Seeing gold allows you to
Appreciate truth
Rise above
Receive your pain
Alchemise your demons
Live
– Living is the real point of gold (and we all have a life and plenty of gold in us)

Gold is like a lightbulb
Just because you aren't looking at it
Doesn't mean you aren't touched by its light
And just because the switch is off
Doesn't mean all the potential isn't right there
And just because all the potential is right there
Doesn't mean you don't need to engage in it to open the floodgates
The more we engage in it,
The more we pack the heat
– Bring the heat, Goldie

'IT' IS GOLD

It is a myth
That you lack gold
A myth
That you will experience
For as long as you believe it
A myth
That you can bust
As soon as you are willing to
– You bust myths by seeing gold

How do I see gold though?
You might ask
And it's a good question
And the answer is
You start
By looking for it
And if you can't see it
You imagine you can
And if you can't see it in someone else
You imagine you can
And if you can't see it in yourself
You imagine you can
You make up all the ways you could be gold
You ask your friends to tell you about your gold
Like on your birthday
Ask for goldenness in your birthday cards
On birthdays
We help our friends see gold
We tell stories
And favourite things
About them
Memories
Love
Laughter
Appreciation
Support
Relief
There's a medicine

It's called the birthday game
We give ourselves this medicine
This reminder
And we give it to each other
Because gold isn't for keeping secret
Gold is a game we are all playing
Gold is all connected
The more we see our gold
The more we see each other's gold
The more we see each other's gold
The more we see our gold
The more we celebrate our gold
The more we shine our gold
The more we shine our gold
The more we remind others of gold
The more we poke at those forgetting their gold
The more opportunities we give for remembering
The more we remember our gold
The more gold our life becomes
The more we relish in our gold
The more the gold spreads
The more the gold spreads
The more happiness
The more fulfilment
The more love
– Are you really trying to tell me that gold isn't the point?

A lesson in gold
Is that it's easy
So if it isn't easy
Whatever you are doing
However you are living
Ask yourself:
Is this simply not gold?
Or am I corrupting the gold? Because you can you know,
Corrupt the gold
You can turn the light off
You can pretend it's not there
You can ignore it
You can procrastinate when you hear it instead of listening
You can avoid the gold
You can be ashamed of the gold
You can be away with the gold
But when you are with the gold
It is easy
All is easy
Even challenges
Nothing stops you
Swift was always going to be a star
Because she felt her gold
And even when others wanted to corrupt it
She didn't let them
And even when she corrupted it
She said enough is enough
And she remembered

She's golden
So she went back to the gold
And now she's so golden nothing can turn off the light
Now she's so golden
She'll be remembered
Her gold will keep spreading
Long after she's here to witness it
The gold grows
The gold expands
And it's easy
Because gold is natural
And gold has momentum
And you bet your bottom dollar
Or even bet your top one!
That gold is the answer
In all your pains
And all your sufferings
There is gold
And when there is gold
There is life
And when life really leads you
It gets to be easy
– Gold blockers are addicted to suffering but you don't have to be

Why does hard work have accolades
And ease gets a bad wrap?
Would you be more impressed by the songwriter who struggles or the songwriter who writes like the breeze?
More impressed by the surgeon who has to force that brain to be there and retain it all or the one who naturally remembers and takes to the human body like a duck to water?
It is nature at work
When the gold moves us
And nature isn't working hard
It's working in alignment
It's working in flow
It's taking what it needs and leaving the rest
It's blooming and shedding as required
And what if we could do that to our careers?
– Then we could live in the gold

'IT' IS GOLD

Nature nature nature
Gold gold gold
Love love love
One one one
– Do you get it yet?

When you're sleeping on my shoulder
And the whole world keeps moving
And my whole world is right here
And suddenly I am called to write
And poetry flows out of me
And songs play in my mind
And love pours out of cells
And ideas flow
And everything is connected
And I want to write it down
And I'll do it one handed, with my left hand,
Because my right one is trapped with you,
Lost in your cuddle
And it is so slow
And I don't care
Because there is no hurry when the whole world is full of gold
– Life with your person is gold

When you go to a different country
And the food is different
And the vibe is different
And the language is different
And the climate is different
And the hotels are different
And the way of life is different
And the etiquette is different
And the price is different
And the colour is different
And the hair is different
And the clothing is different
And the music is different
And the hugs land differently
And the smiles are the same
The love is the same
And you are held the same
And you are human the same
– Gold is universal

When a song comes on
Or a smell floats in
And you remember
A whole other time
A whole other place
A whole other moment
And the whole world has shifted
And then the song ends
Or the smell dissipates
And you're still here
– Gold is time travel

There's a nice man
A lovely man
A generous man
A sad man
And he works 'here'
And it doesn't matter where 'here' is
But the point is
It isn't his gold
It isn't the place where he most brightly shines
And he knows this
But he doesn't see his gold
Not really
He doesn't get that he has this big gold
That if he listened to his big gold
He could live a bigger life
And it matters
Not because it's everyone's truth to live a big life
Of course it isn't
It can be true to live in the forest
To live quietly
For small to be your big
For simple to be your big
But for him
The gold is big
He wants a big life
He is called to a big life
He celebrated my big life
But he couldn't see

That he could have his big life too
– Gold is yours for the taking and you have to take it

'IT' IS GOLD

There's a place
That we can go to
Where the ego cannot come
The pain cannot enter
And only the soul can speak
Only the heart can call out
Only the best stories are told
And they are the stories of your future
Your golden future
(if you let them be)
And you'll receive information
You'll receive the light of who you are
Guidance on the truth of who you are
Reality about the gold of who you are
It will feel like a trip
And like a remembering
And like the most important thing you've ever done
Because it's the moment you see your golden life so clearly
And once you see it
There's no unseeing it
And once you declare you want it
You start acting like it
And once you start acting like it
The golden life starts to come to life
And once the gold takes hold
It doesn't take long to shine brighter
Because the golden life has momentum
The golden life is contagious

The golden life is yours for the choosing

And the first step

Is to be willing

To go to the place

To see all the gold

And then

The golden road will appear

– You go to the gold first, then it will speak to you if you will listen

There is a way of life
That is available to you
Where you put down logic
Not completely
Because yes
You do have to be at the departure gate to board your plane
But no
Not completely
Because you do need to put one foot in front of the other
And get dressed in the morning when you leave the house
Most of the time
But also
You don't have to do what you've always done
And you don't have to go just because you said so
And you don't have to graduate just because it's the done thing
And your job doesn't have to be what you think it is meant to be
And you don't have to base your life off other people's wishes
And you don't even have to base your life off past you's wishes
And you don't have to wear makeup like everyone else
And you don't have to buy a house like everyone else
And you don't have to be a tourist like everyone else
And you don't have to do anything you wouldn't love to
And sometimes it is uncomfortable
And sometimes it is your intuition against the world
And sometimes your mum won't get it
And sometimes your best friend won't come
And sometimes the person you love will reveal painful colours
And sometimes people will believe in you beyond what you imagined

And sometimes the world will bend to you as if by magic
And sometimes the most illogical decision is the best one
And sometimes you just know and you can't explain it
And sometimes the most expensive isn't the best
And sometimes the bargain really is the light
And sometimes you leap before you figure it out
And you have to leap when it's your truth
And you have to run when you see the way
And you have to act when you see the next step
And you have to speak when there's truth to be told
And you have to write when you are called to
And you have to sing despite your stage fright
And you have to invest even when it's uncomfortable
And you have to say yes even if you don't like it
And you have to allow your intuition to guide you regardless of your opinion
And you have to let go of who you have been
To become who you were born to be
To let nature guide you
To reawaken and nurture your inner knowing
To remind yourself over and over again that yes, you can see the truth even if others are hiding
To learn as you go
To pick yourself up when you fail
To get used to failure being a success too
To get used to not knowing all the answers and just knowing this moment
To get invested in enjoying the journey

To get attached to end results and not conditions
To say yes when you are called to
To say no when you are called to
To break the boundaries that aren't serving you
The boundaries of your conditions
The boundaries of your perceived limitations
The boundaries of your self doubt
And place the boundaries of your creativity
The boundaries of your fuck yes life
The boundaries of your standards and your level
And choose
To create a life you love
There is a way
And it's not the done way
Otherwise everyone would be doing it
But it is a natural way
And it is here for your choosing
And it starts by you declaring
'There is more for me than this,'
And then it continues by you sharing that wish
Over and over again
Until you find your way
And you find your people
And you find your process that works
And you find your land of plenty everywhere you look
Because you chose gold
And gold isn't the way of today's society
But it could be the way of tomorrow

And it could be the way of you
If you let it
– Gold isn't the only way but it's a happy one

Other people may tell you
'It's a distraction'
'You can't monetise that'
'You don't know what you're doing'
'I tried it and it doesn't work'
'I tried and failed and so will you'
'You can't do that'
'You said you wouldn't'
'I thought you weren't going to'
'This is not what I expected'
'I am disappointed'
'You are not good enough'
'It's not worth it'
'That's an outrageous investment'
'Your art sucks'
'This sucks - you doing this sucks'
'It's not safe'
'You'll lose everything'
'But you worked so hard for what you already have'
'But you always said you wanted something else'
'But, but, but...'
A million things
Other people may say a million things
And it might be because they care
And it might be because they don't understand
And it might be coming from 'the right place'
And it might be because they think they know what's best
And it might be because they are in pain

And it might be because they are afraid
And it might be because they are jealous
And it might be because they are making it about themselves
But it won't be because they're seeing you as powerful
And it won't be because you have to listen to them
But it will be your choice as to your next move
And your next move will determine your path
And your path is yours is for the taking
And your path is yours for the laying
And your path is yours for enjoying
And your path
IS
YOUR
PATH
So who cares what other people say?
People walking other people's paths
People pretending their path is for someone else
No
It isn't
Your path is your path
Your path is going to serve others
But it's not for others
Your path is for your heart
And you are the only person who can choose it
– Gold is a choice worth making others uncomfortable for

What if nothing mattered?
What if nothing you did created any ripple?
And everything you did meant nothing?
And nothing you did cost anything?
And everything you did felt easy?
And everyone loved you no matter what?
And your friends encouraged you always?
And your loved ones understood you completely?
And your decisions were met with unconditional support always?
And everything you chose was met with validation?
And nothing you could do could take away that validation?
It's called sovereignty
And you guessed it
It's yours for the taking
– Sovereignty is gold

It is gold.

I didn't get it
The medicine
To some
Poison
To others
I didn't get it
I didn't research it
I didn't think about it much
It was simple
– Gold told me not to

'IT' IS GOLD

It wasn't about
Whether they wanted it
Or whether I wanted it
Or whether I was able
Or capable
Or magic
Or mundane
Or whatever
It was about one thing
– Gold told me to

I didn't care about it
A new car
A flashy car
A luxury car
A showy car
A rich mum car
But then I got it
And it all made sense
And I felt like myself
– It is good to be gold

'IT' IS GOLD

'It will feel so abundant owning your own home.'

I could feel it when he said it
My teacher
My friend
But I didn't get it until I lived there
I didn't get it 'til I walked through
Past the giant bow on the door
I didn't get it
Until I did
I think that's how it works
– How gold works is you don't have to understand gold

When I think about 'it'
'It' doesn't make sense
'It' doesn't feel possible
'It' feels like a fantasy
'It' feels like what everyone else says
And what no one else says
'It' feels like a pipe dream
The type that you think is going to come true
And so you don't do anything about it
And then it doesn't
And then you think
I'm not gold
And you're wrong
Because it only didn't come true
Because you didn't do anything
And had you acted the path
You would have reached the end
You would have had 'it'
You would have lived 'it'
You would have learnt the lessons of moving towards 'it'
And then you would have become 'it'
– You could be golden if you acted like it

'IT' IS GOLD

I can see it in the paint
Outside on the street
The words melting in the rain
The cracks drying in the heat
I can see it through the windows
Of the tainted coffee shop
In the art they make on lattes
And the way their faces pop
When they're cast right in the sunlight
And they think no one is watching
And they do dance steps under the table
Like magical hop-scotching
It's crazy how easy it can be
If you really take a look
I see it in all people
And every character in every book
Even in the evil guy
I look and go, 'Wow, he couldn't see it'
And I don't even shame it,
I don't say it's a shame
I learn
And I remind myself
To receive it
Because the gold that lives inside my heart
Is just as visible as yours is
And it's just as loud
And expressive
And awesome

And elusive when I'm being an ass-hat
But when I'm myself,
Which is most of the time
And psssst—secret—that's how I see yours
It's easier to choose
Even when I don't want to
For I've seen all these examples of losses
I've seen all these people
All these places
All these whispers
Of what if
And maybe when...
And I just scream
NO
It shakes up my insides
I can't imagine
THERE MIGHT NOT BE A WHEN!
NOW IS WHEN
You are golden now
Can't you see it?
Open your eyes
Stop trying
Be yourself
It isn't worth hiding
Hiding hurts more than it protects you
Protecting yourself from being yourself doesn't make sense
Nobody cares
Just be you

'IT' IS GOLD

I want to see your art
I'll buy your art
People will buy your art
People will love you for who you are
People will be repelled no matter what
Not everybody gets it
Who cares? You get it
Get it
Please
Just get it
Get that being you is enough.
Get that you are whole.
Get that you are love.
– The truth about gold

'I always wanted to write a book.'
My grandmother
The most wise

And fierce
And sharp
And savage
Woman
And yet she didn't
– You'll miss your gold if you don't live it

'I wrote a poem that was in a book.'
My grandmother again
Years later

She pulls it out
I read it
I'm touched
Tears

'You should write your book, Nan.'

Maybe she will
She's ninety now
And she still has now to write
– Gold is a lineage, living it is a choice

The most beautiful singing voice
My nan
It's where I got it from
Apparently
I've seen everybody can sing
Some sing gold
And certainly there is singing of all the colours of the rainbow
Make that mean what you will
We can all sing
All our souls have a voice
All our souls sound different
All our voices look different on paper
This is my voice
Hers was so beautiful
I'm glad I heard it
– Live with your golden voice, don't die with it

There was a baker
In France
The first time I ever went
We drove in
And there it was
A bakery
I'd never seen one so plain looking
And so magic feeling
And I begged Clare to stop
It didn't take convincing
My first French croissant
From a female baking
And she smiled when she heard our accent
Laughed at our order
Doubled it straight into the bag
She was right
– She baked gold

There was a man
Who sat in the office
At the basketball court
And he didn't know it
Or maybe he did
But he was humble
And he gave us all a sport we loved
In his spare time
And in his passion
And in his tears
We played
And we couldn't have otherwise
And maybe that's simple
But
– Maybe that's gold

'IT' IS GOLD

'I'm so sorry,'
Said mother.
She couldn't do it anymore,

She couldn't stay
She didn't know
She didn't have the glue
She didn't want to
She didn't know how
She didn't get the help she needed when she'd needed it,
She left.

'You were so brave,'

I told her
Because she chose herself
And that's the kind of mum I'm proud to have
– Gold tells you to choose you

'I didn't love her anymore.'
That's fine,
That's allowed.

That's your prerogative
That's your business
That's your excuse
That's your truth
That's yours.
My mistake
Was that I let the lies you told me become mine.
– Gold tells the truth

It's on me
To choose my path
When it presents itself
And it does,
Over and over again
It presents itself
Even when I wander off
And start beating trolls
In the woods
And I've lost the path
And I can't find my way
A golden angel appears
And says, 'Come'
And points, 'This way'
And states, 'Here is a choice'
And sings, 'If you'd like to you can'
And finally
I follow the angel back to the path
And there's still trolls on the path
But they are my healing
They are my remembering
They are my friends
And the trolls in the woods
I don't need them
But the path
Oh my path
It is a freedom like no other to walk there
To run there

It all feels like flying
Even when there's trolls
Definitely when there's golden trolls
I wouldn't have it any other way
– The way is gold, Gold is The Way.

'IT' IS GOLD

When I am afraid
I turn to gold
When I am excited
I relish the gold
When I am calm
I am one with the gold
When I am lost
I seek the gold
When I am together
I share the gold
When I am alone
I still see the gold
When I am loving
I am spreading the gold
When I am yelling
I can't see the gold
And when I whisper
The gold appears
When I am silent
The gold collapses
Or the gold engulfs
And what I've learnt
In all emotion
And all moments
Is that gold is there
– If only I am willing to see it is gold

You know 'it'
You have 'it'
Your gifts and talents are wrapped in 'it'
Your awesome qualities are dripping with 'it'
Your love is laced in 'it'
Your heart is 'it'
Your heart is 'it'
Your heart is 'it'
– You have a heart full of gold

'How do you know when it's *really* gold?'
Well
How do you know when life is shit?
– Gold is *gold*, obviously

I don't want to
But my heart says yes
I am scared to
But my heart says yes
I would love to (if it goes well)
So yes,
I guess
– It is gold

'IT' IS GOLD

'I want to be among the mountains'

Okay.

'Where no car can go'

Okay.

She's an explorer
She sees the world
Through naked eyes
– It is gold

My dad says he loves me
In every comment
He's never shy
With his affections
He has his flaws
As we all do
But oh
He sprinkles love
– It is gold

'IT' IS GOLD

My mother tells me
I love that you dance
Like you do on the beach
Free
Laughing
Wonder in your lungs
She sees me
– It is gold

My mother checks
'Are you okay?'

My grandfather asked
'Are you making money?'

My grandmother asks
'How is Clare?'

My uncle asks
'What are you working on now?'

I hear
Are you safe?
Are you happy?
Do you know you are cared for?
We see your art.
– It is gold

'IT' IS GOLD

When nobody understands it
And you have to do it
Because your heart says so
When nobody has ever been there
And you have to go
Because your heart demands it
When nobody expected this from you
Including yourself
But you had to make it
Because the soul of life willed it from you
When everything is crumbling
And you know everything is still okay
When nobody has the answers
And nobody needs to
When everything is coming together
And you can see clearly now
When you finally did it
And even you are surprised by how great it is
When you get the feedback that you dreamt of
And it's kinda surreal but completely real
When you followed that ludicrous guidance
Because you don't know a lot
But you know enough to listen to your heart
And miracles happen
When all your dreams come true
And then you realise there are more dreams for dreaming
When you are alive and well
And you realise right here and now was the whole point

When you are dancing like nobody's watching
And you realise you are completely free
When you create what you were looking for
And you realise you were led by magic
You will know
That you are one
And you are you
And you?
Are gold.
– You are the gold you've been asking for

Wishing Gold
The Epilogue

There is nothing wrong with wishes
They are not the desperation of hope
Or a power outside oneself
They are a reminder
Of anything you've ever wanted
And that you can have it
If only you will bring it back into your focus
And so
I wish
For you to see your gold
I wish for you to remember
The gold you used to see so naturally
Before you learnt to see grey
For there was a time
Where all you saw was golden
And all you knew was golden
And everywhere you felt love
And you were connected to everything through all of time and space
And you knew it
You knew that you weren't separate
Until you learnt to be separate
And being separate isn't all grey and beige
There's brilliance in your uniqueness
There's magic in knowing who you are
There are your gifts and talents
There is everything you've never known that you will discover
There's acknowledging that you don't know, that brings you closer to your discovery

There's individuation
And you do need to be an individual to be you
Your body is yours
Your emotions are yours
Your life is yours
And yes
They are separate to others
But that separation gets grey when you don't acknowledge your gold
That separation becomes lonely instead of sovereign
It becomes a terror instead of a chosen journey into the wild
So I wish you could remember
(and I know you can)
So I wish you do remember
All that wonderful gold in you
– That wonderful gold in your heart

I wish you could see

The way the gold sings from your skin

The way it drips off you like honey

The way your smile is so contagious

The way the swing of your hips is a siren call of power

The way you connect people with people

The way you see the truth

The way you slice through the bullshit

The way you laugh

Oh,

The way you laugh

I wish you could see the look in your eyes when you see a human you love

Or the way your soul moves you when your favourite song comes on

Or the way your shoulders shake when you sob and let grief move you

Oh I wish you could see

The way your presence uplifts a space

And the way your gifts dance on the shoulders of giants

And the way you are a giant

And the way your love gives and gives

Oh I wish you could see

That in every cell of yours

There is golden

Magic

Golden

'IT' IS GOLD

Magic
Golden
Magic
Gold.
– Oh, You

I wish you knew your gold

Like the way you remember your childhood postcode

Or the way you remember your best friend's favourite pizza

Or the way you remember to take a deep breath at the end of a big day

I wish you knew your gold

In the way you naturally touch your face without thinking

In the way you sit down and immediately wriggle around to get comfortable

In the way you laugh and smile and encourage the one you love as though they can do anything

I wish you knew your gold

As simply as you knew your favourite breakfast

As simply as you knew the joy of freshly washed sheets

As simply as you knew your favourite scent

I wish you knew your gold

So it could be the space you return to

It could be the memory you linger in

It could be the frequency you wash yourself with

It could be the grounding force in your life

And I wish you knew your gold

I wish for you to know your gold

Better now

Deeper now

To recognise your gold

Clearly now

Effortlessly now

And to have the people around you reflect to you your gold

Quickly now

'IT' IS GOLD

Wonderfully now
Without knowing how
Because it isn't about how you know
It's about realising that you already know
You are already gold
Even if you've only been seeing grey
It doesn't make you any less gold
– I wish you knew and I wish you'd tell yourself again and again

Gold is the greatest wish
I have for all of humanity
That when that little girl grows up
And all those people didn't believe in her
Have found their gold
And recovered
And all those people who did believe in her
Have realised that was their gold and play
And have fulfilled their gold
And flourished
I wish that little girl knew
When she was forgetting
That she'd come back
That she'd always find her gold
That she'd always remember her gold
And do you know what?
I think all of my wishes have come true
I think you know your gold
I think you know your wishes are golden
I think you wish gold for others
I think you wish gold for yourself
And I know
That little girl is living in the gold
Because that little girl
Golden or grey
Is you
As much as she is me
– We are all on the golden journey home

fire body warm
out march 2025

A taste of FIRE

When the heat comes
It may drip slowly and steaming
Like lava
Down your chin to your hips
Or it may rise
Like the ocean tides
From your toes to your fingertips
Or it may crackle
Like the charcoal warming the hearth
With all the potential for explosion
And all the safety of enclosure
As it warms you from the middle
And threatens to explode
Or it may dance
Like a flame licking alcohol
And a breeze across your neck
As it stands your hairs on end
And tickles you open

ELLIE ANN DEIGHTON

It matters less
How the heat comes
And matters more
That the heat comes
And oh when the heat comes
You will know
– When the fire starts to burn

Not all fires are equal
Read *fire body warm* from March 2025

About the author

She teaches humans how to live in the light of their true selves and she goes first.
Like an integrity radar
Through life
Hers and yours
She will find the cracks
And spit them out
Until your world tastes like honey together
For she is not here to walk alone
And neither are you.
It is no mistake that you are here reading this.
Is it stories in her books calling you in for a journey?
Is her music singing you home to the temple of you?
Is her curriculum asking you to become more of yourself?
Is now the time?
I believe so.
The scientist in her has a hypothesis,
That you are magic,
The facilitator in her
Can prove it,

The witch in her

Can give you the tools to cast it,

The woman in her

Can celebrate you as you shine,

The artist in her

Is on stage creating beside you.

You are magic,

And here,

You will find that you are home.

– about Ellie, the author of ***'It' is Gold***

Author's note

You are never alone
Because you will always be with gold
And gold will always be with you
And you can close your eyes and see the gold
And you can open your eyes and look for the gold
And you can place your hands on your chest and feel the gold
And you can sing a song and hear the gold
And even on the darkest days
There can be a light
Because of the gold
And the greatest gift you could ever give yourself
Is to learn to

See

Listen

Feel

Receive

Remember

Play

Speak

Be

ELLIE ANN DEIGHTON

Gold
– Gold is what I teach

And I can teach you gold too
Or you can receive little golden drops to your inbox

Subscribe to 'Gold' at elliedeighton.com/gold

Acknowledgements

Clare
Mem
Mum
Dad
Luke
Elise
Elijah
Noah
Daphne
Anthony
Peggy
Zaylee
David
Kirsty
Michael
Karen
Kate
David
Debbie
Alex

William
Paige
Elissa
Alaina
Taylor
The Scottish Highlands
Corfu
– Thank you for being golden, ***'It' is Gold*** wouldn't exist without you